OFFICE KAMA SUTRA

Contents

In writing down these secret truths,
I may have erred and made myself uncouth.
But if lovers find pleasure through my
              small efforts,
And no one is offended, harassed,
              or put out of sorts,
Then none can say it was a bad thing
To bring romance to the land where fax
              and modem sing.

FOR THE SECRET LOVERS OF
THE CUBICLE WORLD, AND FOR "STAN"

My thanks to all who helped in the creation of Office Kama
Sutra, *especially Erin McMahon and her libidinous friends for
their suggestions and anecdotes, Sushma Patel for kindly reading
an early draft, Sarah Malarkey for her inspiration, and Derek
Chen for his diligence as a fact checker. Thanks also to designer
Pamela Geismar, illustrator Thorina Rose, and editor Beth
Weber for their many contributions, made with good cheer.*

Text copyright © 2001 by Julianne Balmain
Illustrations copyright © 2001 by Thorina Rose

Library of Congress Cataloging-in-Publication Data available.
ISBN 0-8118-3138-8
Printed in Singapore.

Designed by Pamela Geismar

Distributed in Canada by Raincoast Books
9050 Shaughnessy Street
Vancouver, British Columbia V6P 6E5

10 9 8 7 6 5 4 3 2 1

Chronicle Books LLC
85 Second Street
San Francisco, California 94105

www.chroniclebooks.com

Office Kama Sutra

BEING A GUIDE TO
DELECTATION & DELIGHT
IN THE WORKPLACE

By Julianne Balmain
Illustrations by Thorina Rose

CHRONICLE BOOKS
SAN FRANCISCO

Translator's Note

The only extant copy of the original *Office Kama Sutra* is rumored to have been discovered in 1952 in the basement of a defunct Bombay shipping bureau by a lawyer closing escrow on the site. Alas, flipping through the manuscript, he spotted *coitus, seminal eruption,* and *yoni* in suspicious proximity to *accounts ledger, payroll,* and *Dictaphone* and swiftly resolved to dispose of the salacious treatise. Seizing its pages one after the other, he thrust them into the coal burner with furtive zeal. It is said that future generations have the shipyard owner himself, at the time well over 120 years of age, to thank for rescuing what is left of the work, as it was he who rushed in at the first whiff of burning love.

We may never know what was lost due to the hasty judgment of the solicitor's flames, though it is likely to have been the chapters on advanced and occult practices, since he launched his attack from the rear. What was left was translated into Gaelic and Russian, and in the late seventies published in French by a vanity press serving the exotic needs of a handful of anonymous sponsors. Now at last, English-language readers have access to this invaluable text. In translating, every effort has been made to maintain the flavor and intent of the original, while at the same time rendering the overall experience as relevant to modern readers as possible. Where necessary, arcane terminology and references to now-obscure traditions have been preserved out of respect for the integrity of the composition.

Introduction

With the bright sun glinting off freshly scrubbed cheeks, productive individuals arrive at the place of work each morning. Throughout the day, they mingle with their coworkers, separated only by shoulder-high walls that can hardly contain the passion simmering deep within the human breast. They nibble the midday meal together, share pleasantries, commiserate in times of hardship, and gather frequently to converse on urgent business matters. They may even travel to distant cities for business-related sojourns. Inevitably, desire is awakened and they must ask the ancient question, "Shall we do it or not? This way or that?" The answers are to be found in the pages of *Office Kama Sutra*.

As is recorded by the sages of old, men and women have 100 years in which to fulfill their destiny, 100 years being the natural duration of a human life. Of these years, 20 are spent in youth and 20 in old age. Of the remaining 60, four decades are devoted to amassing wealth, and those being the most fruitful segment of the 100, wise men and women will multitask and pursue *kama* (sensual pleasure) simultaneously with the pursuit of *artha* (land, gold, cattle, and other such material gain). The wise speak thusly knowing that after toiling long hours at the exchange of goods or the cultivation of yams and cumin, the mind is addled with practical concerns and indisposed to amorous thoughts. When the sun is fallen low and the briefcase grown heavy like an ox's burden, what lover has strength to perform the dance of seduction around a potential paramour with adequate stamina and vigor? Who has had time to gather the appropriate herbs, prepare the necessary poultices, and still manage to compose a lyrical ballad before the stars reveal their enflamed gaseous presence? Few are those who can manage it. More common is the lover who, made ardent to the point of near obsession by daily proximity, finds that the tempting fruit dangling so near cannot but be seized and devoured, even though the risks are great and the convenience store nearby is well stocked with succulent treats to be had risk-free and at a discount. Logic does not govern the realm of *kama*.

Eight hours of the day (not counting lunch), five days of the week, the worker toils, longing to be transfigured by the warm, sweet trade winds of love. Accordingly, the techniques and arts of romance at the office are referred to as the 40 Ways. Certainly there may be more than 40—the nephew of the learned author Varāhamihira claimed to have mastered at least 60—yet still they are called the 40 Ways, for the 40 hours each week during which they are practiced. One may be at the office more than 40 hours or less, and still the arts of office *kama* are known as the 40 Ways.

In truth, why *not* pursue the love arts while at work, where so many of life's joyful days are spent? For if a worker refrains from copulation and shuns

the 40 Ways, devoting him- or herself solely to the pursuit of wealth until the heat of the fiery sword has diminished with the years, or until Cupid's den has grown hoary with disuse, then no matter the prosperity of the worker's household, the obstacles to love will be many and the passion of coition greatly impeded by a lack of practical experience.

Further, life is uncertain; death or misfortune may arrive unannounced. Therefore, it is prudent to seize upon opportunity in all instances. As the great man of letters Vātsyāyana has written, "A pigeon to eat is worth more than a peacock in the sky." Casting a judicious glance over the cubicle farm and perusing the office's sundry visitors, what champion of industry does not espy a tasty morsel worthy of pursuit?

Love and work will spring up from the same fertile ground, but how to proceed? As in the commerce of goods and services, so in the commerce of love must workers be vigilant and wary, always seeking to epitomize the seven noble graces. By balancing temperance with desire, and by following the wisdom of *Office Kama Sutra*, so will a worker reap the harvest of well-cast seed, both professionally and romantically.

PART ONE

Selecting a Promising Vocation and Workplace

When a supple-skinned youth reaches the age of the ripened mango fruit and it is time to choose a vocation, consideration should be given to *kama* (pleasure) as well as *artha* (wealth). For while there are many means of acquiring material goods, some jobs are more suited to amorous pursuits than others. Certain careers, even those without offices, are known to abound in opportunties. These include traveling tinker or salesperson, professional athlete, and, in certain instances, holy man or woman. Others—midwife or surgeon, real estate agent, psychologist, masseuse, politician, horse trainer—serve up pleasures of the flesh with such frequency that participants risk over-satiation.

Most Desirable Careers

For those whose desire charges ahead like a wild boar and whose taste for the ambrosia of coition is never sated from morning to night, there is no better entrée to the joys and mysteries of the 40 Ways than the role of bike messenger, postal worker, or other delivery personnel. Delivery folk are well liked in general, being the bearers of packages and the trusted envoys of vital documents. Bike messengers are further favored for their dash, adventurous spirit, and asceticism; overnight delivery drivers for their admirable swiftness; and postal carriers for their constancy and companionship. Aside from enjoying daily travel and free access to a wide variety of organizations, delivery personnel routinely engage in pleasant, flirtatious banter with temporary employees, mail clerks, and receptionists, who are themselves the next best choices for young workers with a fire blazing in their loins.

When indulging in office *kama,* one cannot do better than the temporary assignment. Temporary workers, including the myriad varieties of business consultants, assume the cloak of anonymity and, like a soft breeze carrying the scent of honeysuckle

Delivery Personnel Are Well Liked in General

over a garden wall, glide hither and yon at will, tickling the nostrils in passing. A choice arrangement, their presence is made all the more appealing by the threat of their imminent departure, and their temporary status ensures ease of exit should complications arise. Often, they must collaborate with permanent employees, meeting in bare conference rooms, their fingertips almost touching over a yellow notepad, the waft of cologne and body mist heavy in the air, brows furrowed in concentration as their minds race toward forbidden thoughts.

The following anecdote is told of Gonikā-putrayana the garland maker. Due to a lifetime of unusual circumstances, he found himself without a lover. Though several toothsome peers at the garland factory fluttered their lashes when he passed, his scrupulousness prevented him from action. Lonely, increasingly despondent, Gonikāputrayana toiled and the years passed until one day when the inventory manager went on vacation and was replaced by Anūdhā, a temporary worker of notable charm. Gonikāputrayana said to himself, "Surely I am not the sort of snake charmer to hang affectionately but inappropriately on the sari of a coworker?" And so he waited with barely restrained impatience for the inventory manager's two-week vacation to pass. As the temporary replacement walked toward the exit door after her final day, Gonikāputrayana, who had enhanced his costume that day with several fragrant garlands, slyly passed before her, tugging his right ear auspiciously. Anūdhā was perplexed by this behavior and shyly asked Gonikāputrayana if it meant he would like to partake of refreshing fruity beverages at a nearby café. Not long after, they shared an embrace of unsurpassed and enduring sweetness.

Not all men and women can be temporary employees or consultants, but that is no cause for despair. For those willing to proceed cautiously and with great attention to protocol, other roles can suffice. The virtues of the receptionist's position, for example, are self-evident. A benevolent force of hospitality and greeting, with ready access to employees of every rank, the receptionist is like a favored cousin to whom all feel an immediate attachment. The constant parade of individuals before the receptionist's eyes dramatically increases the likelihood that he or she will identify a suitable mate during the course of the workday.

Receptionist or not, one cannot overvalue the usefulness of incidental contact, whether chatting in the lunchroom or mingling at the otherwise pointless meetings of professional associations. For making a potent betel mixture, one must blend many ingredients, not only cardamom and lime; and for the successful fomentation of passion, one requires contact with many people. When the goal is to entwine like the limbs of jujube trees along a riverbank, variety is fundamental to the cause. Knowing this, the wise lover seeks business relations with an ever-broadening network of associates, both within the corporation and outside of it. If one frequents only a single fruit stall, and this fruit stall does not sell the fragrant pineapple, and one seeks to purchase a fragrant pineapple and nothing else, then one will be disappointed indefinitely. However, if the persistent shopper visits numerous fruit stands at various times, surely one of them will offer such a pineapple and success will be in hand.

Contact need not always be face to face for eyebrows to dance and lips to snarl in a grimace of affectionate mockery. Because distance works like a magic potion to ensnare both parties in Cupid's net, the customer service department is a fruitful abode for lovers. Beneath each sonorous jangle of the telephone and melodious piping of the e-mail announcement lurks the potential for romance. What is not seen is always more enticing than what is known, and telephone and e-mail lovers are likewise more stimulating than their flesh-and-blood counterparts. "Cold calling" is anything but in the hands of those educated in the 40 Ways.

Perhaps the most profitable position of all is that of desktop technical support or information technology worker. They wear the protective and mysterious cloak of technology and are gifted with responsibilities that can keep them at the office late into the night; they enjoy admittance to dimly lit rooms and the freedom to roam the hallways and intrude on any office or cubicle unannounced. They even have access to private correspondence stored on networks and hard drives. Enjoying the mobility of a tomcat and the stealth of the gazelle, the IT worker has been known to attempt exploits of an epic scale without fear of scrutiny or reprisal. When, for example, an IT worker unsuccessfully proposes an after-hours drink, he or she need only mumble such words as "network connectivity" and

The IT Worker Has Ample Opportunity

"binary coding module" a few times while backing slowly away from the offended party, who may not even be aware that woo has been pitched and deflected, but only that some sort of technology-based misunderstanding has occurred. And if their woo lands on fertile ground, there are ample opportunities to lean closely over the paramour while administering to his or her work station.

The last three best roles for the rambunctious virgin or would-be seducer are sales representative, designer, and nightclub singer; the first because the position routinely involves travel, conferences in which long hours of boredom combined with close quarters weaken the participants' defenses, and evening meetings accompanied with savory dishes and fermented beverages; the second because devotion to a craft and artsy wristwatches are universally attractive, and because the ungraspable light of creativity blinds even the least vulnerable associates, rendering them lovesick and complacent in droves; and the third because red candlelight and sequins make any man or woman irresistible. (Karaoke is an acceptable though inferior substitute to an actual career as a nightclub singer.)

Least Desirable Careers

The high visibility of the creative director, while an asset to the nightclub singer or actor, makes maneuvering tricky and the ramifications of failed encounters potentially grave. Likewise, the roles of founder, CEO, and president, while offering unparalleled opportunity for seduction and conquest, are in fact the least desirable positions from the perspective of the lover, for the simple reason that there is too much at stake. Imagine the ramifications of an untoward liaison for a man or woman of high office, particularly if the village press should learn of it. Likewise, métiers in which one functions as a guide, mentor, or confidant to the uninitiated, including those of teacher, professor, therapist, counselor, or human resources manager, are the least profitable means of pursuing office *kama*, since the temptations are many and the risks perilous.

The last undesirable role for those devoted to the science of pleasure is that of the freelancer. While adept at self-manipulation, the freelancer is at a serious disadvantage in the pursuit of office *kama* due to the lack of an office, or if he or she does have an office, due to the typically solitary and domestic

The Lonely Freelancer

conditions therein. Committed freelance workers must take pains to exercise the lingam or yoni on a regular basis and practice initiating the flow of casual conversation, using the photographic likeness of a past coworker or acquaintance if necessary.

Basic Attributes of the Workplace

When searching for love, the place of employment is as important as the type of career one selects. For example, the gardener spends the day surrounded by lush grasses and blue sky, in blissful bowers strewn with petals, and in grottos of tender mosses; but with only mowers, blowers, rakes, and hoes for company, how is a gardener to practice the 40 Ways? A place of work should have at least 20 employees, so as to ensure an ample supply of prospects, but not more than 200, lest anonymity prevail. Further, the position should be favorable and pleasant, but not ideal. The practice of office *kama* is not without risk; better to undertake one's pursuits while in a disposable job, such as apprentice to the ledger keeper, than be forced to terminate a long-term and extremely desirable engagement due to the shabby outcome of a once-promising liaison. While consorts bestow their affection more readily on the powerful, men and women skillful in the 40 Ways need not fear loneliness even if they make their living as a slave or lowly elephant driver.

Other qualities of the superior office include frequent turnover, an equal distribution of yoni to lingam, the opportunity to discuss topics related to sexuality (as at a magazine, advertising agency, catering company, or equestrian center), and a plenitude of secluded spaces (fish hatcheries, circuses, department stores). At minimum, one should make a reasonable effort to acquire keys to the supply or server rooms.

The Lowly Elephant Driver

The 90 Days of Chastity

Opinions about the 40 Ways are as many as cloud formations in springtime, but all intelligent people agree that new hires must observe a period of chastity of not less than 90 days. Mingling is admissible, chatter is tolerated, and the occasional undulation of the hips or tossing of hair is not without merit. However, workers must never seek to consummate a flirtation before the 90 Days have elapsed. Until then, volatile chemistry surrounds the new hire like a benign fog which turns noxious at the first hint of suspicion. There are many disastrous examples of impulsive behavior and its dire consequences in the epic Veda poems. Even in the instance of prolonged and painful abstinence or acute stimulation, the 90 Days must be observed. During this time, reconnaissance activities covering all departments may be conducted and suitable candidates identified, whether by means of an intermediary or through direct contact. Fermented beverages may be consumed in the company of coworkers, but not to the point of drunkenness, or coition may inadvertently occur.

PART TWO

Finding a Suitable Lover

Like a honeycomb noisy with bees, the workplace is abuzz with potential consorts. However, unlike drones laboring at the hive, one's coworkers are far from interchangeable. A lover must be selected with care, and only after much contemplation. The wise do not plunge blindly over the precipice of ecstasy, but observe instead the best route to the beloved from the towering bluffs of good conscience and forethought. Compatibility of both mental and physical makeup is a key concern, as is attraction, personal history, and the roles of both parties at the office in question.

Of Hedgehogs and Hummingbirds

What is the measure of a man's or woman's love? The wise consider the question carefully before courting a potential husband or wife. There are three classifications of Vishnu's sword and three of Pārvatī's tunnel. These relate not only to physical characteristics but also describe the temperament, passion, and preferences of the individual. While there is no inherent virtue to one classification over the other, it is undisputed that the best couplings occur between correlating capacities.

Vishnu's Sword

Those men called hedgehogs can be recognized by a tendency to shuffle papers when nervous. They often have small ears and little hair on their toes and fingers. Their gait is swift, and they excel at games such as squash and cricket. They keep their persons tidy and never wear white socks except to the gym. Hedgehogs are rarely architects, masons, or carpenters, due to their distrust of heights, but are often found at advertising agencies and PR firms.

Those men called brown pelicans are big-boned and lumbering. They laugh like oafs but are astute at geometry, politics, and financial analysis. Their skin is the color of roasted chestnuts and they touch their hair when interested in what is being said. Their nails may be rosy pink or purple, and their thighs and buttocks are well formed. They are often engineers or the captains of shipping vessels.

Men called king salmon are wily and nocturnal. Always smiling, they rarely laugh outright. In conversation, they are decisive and passionate, and prone to heated disputes. Drawn to sales, business development, and the sailing of wooden boats for sport, they wear pointed loafers and their necks are elongated, with a pronounced Adam's apple.

Pārvatī's Tunnel

Women who are called hummingbirds have delicate, glistening skin and white teeth. Their tongues dart about their mouths when they are amused, and they have dark, finely shaped eyebrows. Prone to melodious laughter, they can be heard all the way from the lunchroom when amusing themselves on the telephone at their desk in the marketing department. Watch for scarves the color of summer roses to find a hummingbird woman.

Women called panthers are middling in height and weight. They are robust of spirit, with fingernails shaped like teardrops, and make excellent athletes, controllers, and CFOs. Panther women have a fondness for spicy stews and curries, and are often found near the microwave at lunchtime with plastic containers of savory leftovers in hand. In the games of love, the panther is a formidable and passionate adversary.

The third kind of female is the great bear. Ursine women are voluminous, either physically or sentimentally. Their ampleness and compassion are unsurpassed. Bears tend to have soft hair, high sing-song voices, a fondness for sugary treats, and diminutive toes and fingernails. Adept at finance,

they are especially drawn to men with beards and are beloved by craftspeople and silversmiths.

The hedgehog man fits best with a hummingbird woman, adequately with a panther, and poorly with the great bear. The brown pelican is best matched with the panther, but succeeds adequately with the hummingbird and bear. The king salmon is wise to seek the bear, but can make do with a panther. King salmon must spurn hummingbirds and vice versa, except in the most dire of circumstances. Should a hedgehog fall in love with a bear, a hummingbird with the king salmon, or indeed a hedgehog with a king salmon, all is not entirely lost. In such cases, a rigorous program of calisthenics and large doses of vitamins for the tender parties, and daily meditation, chamomile infusions, and lessons at the harpsichord for the vigorous, will help bridge the gap.

And yet it is not so simple as matching hedgehog and hummingbird or systems engineer with programmer; there are other considerations to ponder when searching for a harmonious partnership. The lover must observe the potential consort's behavior, watching for indications of shyness, audacity, licentiousness, or wrath—all characteristics which require skillful navigation in order to stay the course toward peace and joy. No matter if the object of one's tender affection is aggressive like a silver hawk with sharpened talons or timid like the leaf-eating jungle langur, the lover must learn as much as possible the nature of his or her heart's desire, in order to better fulfill his or her romantic fantasies. This is true even when preparing curry. What use is a cauliflower stew to the woman who craves seasoned eggplant? One must understand the appetite of the beloved.

Those Who Are Easiest and Most Difficult to Seduce

In many cases, the beloved's classification will be less crucial than the lover's statistical potential for success. The well-educated lover understands which kind of person is easiest to seduce and which most difficult. Easiest are those who have observed a lengthy period of abstinence; who are married to persons who live abroad, travel frequently, or have taken a vow of chastity; who are in the habit of reading love stories or drinking fermented beverages to excess; or who spend more than four nights a week at the gymnasium. Most difficult are those who have taken a recent vow of chastity; who are happily married to fecund partners; who show signs of extreme, lasting fatigue; who rise unnaturally early in order to golf before beginning each day; or who spend excessive hours gambling or playing games of whatever sort. Magical potions and spells should not be used on those known to be averse to seduction, lest disappointment or injury result.

The Law of the Direct Report

Having caught sight of the ideal lover, one is eager to skip formalities, burn a chunk of ceremonial amber, and commence the dance of quivering thighs immediately, but celebration must be deferred until it is clear that the love object is neither one's assistant nor boss. This is called the Law of the Direct Report, and it is the unanimous opinion of the enlightened that it must be observed, exceptions being made only in the most extreme cases. From both ethical and practical points of view, relations with one's bosses or subordinates are to be condemned, and copulation with them is strictly forbidden. They will therefore seem the most piquant and savory of delicacies. Add a stimulating disparity in power and authority to the attraction of the forbidden, and it is clear that temptation will be great.

It is acceptable to engage in congress with a direct report only in the dire event that a lover experiences all seven signs of imminent demise from love-sickness, namely:

§ Lack of appetite and emaciation of the body

§ Inability to sleep

§ Rejection of means of former enjoyment, such as playing card games and reciting limericks

§ Excessive propensity to sigh and stare

§ Forgetfulness and dulled wit

§ Lack of will to continue existence outside presence of the love object

§ Inclination to dwell irrationally upon passing conversation and other inconsequential exchanges with beloved, as if said exchanges were of great import

Otherwise, the Law of the Direct Report may be legitimately transgressed only when acute boredom or involuntary abstinence lasts longer than three crop rotations of an ordinary rice field or when a senior coworker has openly done so successfully and without reprimand. Congress with a boss is occasionally practiced by immoral persons in order to enlist a superior's support in retaliation against injurious behavior committed by a third party, to destroy an enemy, or to promote one's own career. Though common in the military and among dancers, musicians, and actors, such behavior is widely considered unethical. Even those who recommend manipulative strategies acknowledge the unpredictable nature of their outcome.

Within their own division or department, employees must jostle the spicy mango cart only with hierarchical peers; however, outside the department, it is possible to eschew the chain of command. For this reason, office *kama* between departments (cross-pollination) is recommended. The most threadbare excuse for a foray into another department should be seized upon by the worthy suitor, and connections with sales, marketing, and business development should be cultivated in the hope of business-related travel. The sales and marketing departments often yield skillful lovers, perhaps due to the extroverted personalities typically found there. However, few men or women have husked the ripe papaya with anyone in sales and marketing without the rest of the organization, and often the trade media, knowing about it. Those who seek discretion go instead to the darkened corridors and shabby offices of research and development, where many timid but passionate souls await discovery. Other departments worth exploring include design, creative, and editorial (flamboyant lovers adept at the advanced arts of promiscuity), finance (cloistered hearts yearning for release), customer service (randy seducers, skillful in telephone and e-mail congress), tech support (sexual wizards predisposed to occult practices), and public relations (instigators of moderate-to-advanced sado-masochism). Legal, human resources, logistics, and operations should be avoided entirely, even in cases of intense mutual infatuation. The litigious and bureaucratic habits of these departments have led to numerous incidents of frigidity, lasting in some cases for decades.

Even better than foraging outside one's department is sampling outside the company walls. Freelancers, clients, and visiting salespeople possess many lovable attributes worthy of admiration. Though their visits may be brief, a sprinkling of ground peanuts will make them feel welcome and talkative. Always offer a finger bowl of cool water with two or three rose petals floating in it for refreshing themselves, and then wait patiently to see if a sparkle of fondness lights up their normally furrowed brow. If nothing happens, offer them a caraway seed cake and move on to the official purpose of the visit.

Or, consider the messenger. Like bees plunging into the flowers' depths, delivery personnel arrive swiftly, bearing gifts. A mist of perspiration moistens their temples, freshly laundered socks grip their robust calves, the scent of the outdoors plays about their person. Seeing them, khaki collar askew and clipboard in hand, few can resist their ample charms. In the case of the bike messenger, their arrival is accompanied with the pleasant tinkling of chains or piercings, while their well-taxed muscles may be decorated with fine etchings and iconography. There is no reason to restrain thoughts of passion when they are near. Being occupied with deliveries and obligations, they are sometimes unable to reciprocate every sugary glance foisted in their direction. Still, a gesture of admiration—pursing of the lips, touching of the forefinger to the inside of the wrist, or slinging the breasts into motion—makes the intent clear to the perceptive.

Consider the Messenger

When All Else Fails

If no harp strings twang after several months on the job, would-be seducers must tie a bundle of cinnamon sticks together with coarse yarn or string and place it beneath their pillow before bed. It should be left in place until the seeker experiences a potently erotic dream about a coworker, but not longer than six nights. If no dream is experienced, the lover has not yet been hired. The committed should wait three months and repeat the process. If no dream occurs the second time, they must wait six months and add a small packet of whole cloves to the cinnamon bundle. Throughout the six months, they should volunteer for all task forces and special teams. No matter how repugnant or dull-witted the dream lover may appear in reality, he or she will be the chosen soul mate.

PART THREE

The Arts of Seduction

While the techniques of seduction are as numerous as starfish in the sea, no single approach is a sure thing. The strategy must be adapted to suit the setting, local customs, and the character of the gentle dove one wishes to court. When a servant lights the hearth fire, he does not always use papyrus. Depending on the season, the condition of the fuel, and his own prejudices, he may use newspaper, twigs, leaves, or dried dung. On certain damp and chilly mornings, he may even resort to lighter fluid. Similarly, some situations call for love notes and sugary tea, others for ribald gyrations and hot masala in order to get started. However, no matter what sort of romance is sought, it is always essential to look one's best.

Hygienic Practices
Are Worth the Effort

Beards and malodorous parts may be the norm on lengthy and arduous pilgrimages and jungle treks, when making war, or while performing grueling tasks such as installing system upgrades or disgorging annual sales figures, but when pursuing the arts of seduction, one must pay close attention to the upkeep of the skin, hair, nails, and teeth. Rising early, the lover should stretch and partake of outdoor sport to keep the body firm and agile, returning in time to bathe, remove excess hair from the face and body, and anoint the skin with purified ghee, yak butter, or a glycerin-based body lotion. The teeth should be polished to a bright sheen, the hair lightly oiled and combed smooth, and enticing fragrances dabbed at the temples, neck, armpits, wrists, groin, and ankles. Sweet almond oil should be rubbed into the nails of the hands and feet, and the eyebrows and eyelashes darkened with charcoal. Chewing blended betel, a stalk of fresh mint, or minty gum to freshen the lips and breath, the worker then departs for the office at an unharried

pace, documents neatly stowed in briefcase or messenger bag, dressed in a comely ensemble with delicate ornaments added, such as gold bangles, fine silk scarves, or necklaces or garlands of jasmine, wisteria, lilac, honeysuckle, or freesia.

In formal business settings, it is customary to lacquer the nails and bottoms of the feet, though in cooler regions where sandals are not worn, the bottoms of the feet are not lacquered. If there are any rough or unsightly areas of the body, they should be rubbed nightly with a mixture of sweet almond oil, warm cocoa butter, and essential oil of vanilla bean, cinnamon, coconut, or sandalwood. The gums should be scoured twice weekly with ashes mixed with betel and cardamom, or at least a fierce mouthwash should be swished behind the lips. On the first day of each lunar cycle the cuticles should be soaked, pushed back, and trimmed. Mustaches, if worn, should be cleaned, trimmed, oiled, and twisted into neat curls every other Sunday in preparation for Monday morning staff meetings.

Decorating the Cubicle, Office, or Company Vehicle

Just as the body is made more appealing with scented oils and fine clothing, so the cubicle, office, or company caravan is made more enticing by ornaments and additions. Wherever possible, those predisposed to practice the 40 Ways should strive to create an appealing décor that others will feel inclined to visit periodically, whether on business or other pretenses. Certain additions to the standard office décor may be necessary, such as tapestries, cushions, and a hookah. If there is adequate space, a sunken sitting area and a fountain's melodious trickling will contribute greatly to a commodious setting. In all cases, the soft musical strains of the lute or vina are highly appropriate, and are especially nice on barges and caravans. Other accouterments may include embroidered cushions and a carved lute in one corner, should anyone wish to play; an array of

Additions to Standard Office Décor

sweets and other small offerings such as gum, hard and chewy candies, nougats, chocolates, mints, nuts, and miscellaneous confections to be eaten with the fingers; and various scented candles. In addition, amorous workers should maintain supplies of (and cultivate a reputation for) small but handy items, such as loose change, floppy disks, postage stamps, tea bags, instant-soup cups, and packets of popular condiments such as ketchup, sugar, and soy sauce, not to mention standard potions to ward off the evil eye or threat of illness.

Dispensing such supplies whenever they are requested fosters goodwill and encourages visits. (Note that it is never appropriate or even desirable to offer mango pickle.) Workers should also keep incense, cotton tissues, a tin of pure yak butter, a selection of pleasantly scented lotions, and a box of lubricated sheep entrails hidden in a safe place in the event of actual office *kama*. A certain area of the office should be devoted to dishes of amber and myrrh. On occasion, a foul odor may inadvertently be emitted—whether evil southern wind or other bodily production—within the walls of the cubicle or office. At such dire moments, it is important to have the countermeasure within reach.

When a guest visits, it is polite to offer candied ginger, peanuts with chili powder, or other comestibles, saying "Please, friend, a morsel of candied ginger for you." If there is a business matter to resolve, it should be addressed and the day's work continued; however, if the visit is a social call, one may play the lyre briefly or entertain the guest with a truncated version of the dance of welcome before returning to work. In the afternoon, it is not out of the question to amuse oneself and others for a short period of time by training the office mynah birds and parrots to say witty phrases.

On Not Being an
Impudent Woodcock

If a certain coworker visits one's space numerous times during the day, whether under the auspices of work matters or not, it is apparent that he or she is preoccupied by the 40 Ways. Still, one must not make love immediately. It is far better to wait until desire has built up like a dark cloud grown heavy with moisture than to straddle the occupant unawares, like the unannounced assault of a monkey dropping out of a tree. One must not lunge at the peachy buttocks or grope the buttery mounds of breasts uninvited, nor engage in *frottage* with passing hips and legs until a proper foundation of mutual affection has been firmly established. Those who do so are no better than an impudent woodcock. Such discretion also applies to the licking and sucking of toes; one must never lick or suck coworkers' toes without preamble.

Aiming for decorum and discretion at all times, lovers should attempt to verify that the frequent visitor is indeed amorous. If he or she flutters the lashes and looks away at the floor or wall in

Checking In

one's presence, that is good evidence that the party in question is smitten. If they sigh frequently, cough, grow pale or blush red, twist their hair, bite or chew their lips or fingertips, dig their hands into their pockets, linger pointlessly, or laugh without sufficient provocation in one's presence, visitors are clearly smitten. Also, they may be smitten if their manner of dress, personal hygiene, or arrangement of the hair noticeably improves without other explanation. When a phone call or e-mail would suffice, and yet they choose to climb two flights of stairs in order to pay a visit, randy Cupid has surely trained his arrow on their heart. Sending extraneous e-mails rife with familiarity also indicates affection, as does forwarding amusing voice mails to one's telephone extension. When in doubt, the man or woman who pokes his or her head around the corner near the close of the workday in order to smilingly "touch base" one last time before heading home, when combined with weekly or daily invitations to lunch together, whether alone or in a group, is exhibiting signs of love. If numerous indicators are present and still one is timid with fright and uncertainty, one must observe the hands and feet of the beloved, especially during meetings. When hands sway like elephant grass ruffled by a stiff breeze, when the foot rocks and glides like a reed canoe at anchor, when the fingers graze the laptop keyboard delicately like a cloud passing over a tall building, then tenderness and gentle caresses are not far in the future.

Knowing the dangers of office *kama*, the wise put a new lover to numerous tests before plunging into the affair like a hippopotamus splashing into an inviting green river. Perhaps late one afternoon, as often occurs, the beloved lingers in one's office before departing, snacking from dishes of toasted cashews and almonds. Many have been the signs of their devotion. In such an instance, the lover looks up at the beloved, smiling, lips parted slightly with barely contained passion, visions of fantastic couplings playing in the mind's eye, and says, "Want to get a beer?"

Elevators, Meetings, and Other Public Spaces

It is safe to assume that lovers, once free from the restrictions and unflattering lighting of the corporate setting, will lose no time in commencing with heartfelt embraces. Later, their secret burns inside them like a glowing ember, and hardly can they pass each other in the hallway without a knowing glance. When they meet coincidentally at the coffee station or copier, they struggle to repress smiles, giggles, and tender or playful gestures. Repressing these impulses, their love grows all the stronger, like steam trapped in a cauldron of simmering rice. Every contact between them fuels their mutual lust and admiration, and they seize any opportunity for contact, however brief. In the elevator, when the two lovers stand silently with other workers present, and one of the lovers brushes his or her fingers

Zebras in a Herd of Gazelles

against the hand, thigh, or wrist of the other lover unbeknownst to the fellow workers, it is called "the embrace of the grazing fingers," or "zebras in a herd of gazelles." When the boy, seeing the girl walk by and noting her shadow on a wall, leaps from his chair to kiss the place where her shadow passed, it is called "the embrace of the distracted butterfly." When together they conspire to escape for a few moments under the pretext of fetching sacks of seed for the office mynah birds, picking up reproductions from the local copy shop, or some other errand, it is called "two thieves capering in moonlight."

During meetings, the two romancers should take care not to sit next to each other, lest they lose control or forget themselves, placing a fingertip on the wrist, bestowing a small kiss on the cheek, or tenderly pushing a strand of hair back from their lover's brow. When the dalliance is new, only with difficulty is the mind torn away from the delicious love grotto. How many times has a question been put to the newly fallen, who looks up from his or her notepad like a cow interrupted from grazing, without any idea of the topic of conversation, let alone the question being asked? Swiftly he or she regains composure, saying, "It's certainly an issue

The Dance of Wayward Toes

that deserves consideration. But it shouldn't delay any of the final deliverables."

In large meetings with lengthy agendas and many attendees, where distraction is tolerated and even courted, "the dance of wayward toes" makes an excellent diversion. More often, however, large meetings are a stage upon which the lovers must act out their professional roles, ever fearful that their coworkers will glimpse evidence of their secret liaison. At such times, Freudian slips (*sex* for *six*, *yearnings* for *earnings, analist* for *analyst*), blushing, and inappropriate erection of the nipples or lingam all pose significant threats to the lover's reputation. As a precaution against such exposure, lovers should avoid standing at the white board and should carry props such as large folders, laptop computers, and clipboards to hide behind, and wear trousers with pockets, bulky or oversized jackets, and binding camisoles as appropriate. Both hero and heroine should refrain from whispering or making direct eye contact unless they wish everyone present to know of their dalliances.

Mastery of the Telephone and E-Mail Arts

Many are the joys of talking with a lover on the telephone. The voice ripples like chimes when the lover calls, and the most mundane of exchanges becomes titillating, which is why it must be avoided as much as possible at the office. All will surmise that one is talking with a lover, even if the words betray nothing. Everything is in the love song of the voice, sweet like frothed milk and honey. And if, in an effort to maintain the ruse, the lover does not respond in sweetnesses but behaves as though the caller were nothing more than a passing goatherd requesting fodder, then the cherished caller may become dispirited and lackluster, crestfallen at the lack of enthusiasm transmitted from mouthpiece to receiver. In such a case, it may be necessary to spend an entire evening reassuring the beloved of one's dedication. If the lovers are adamant about using the telephone, a safe and amusing game is to repeatedly dial the extension of the beloved, and when he or she answers to say, "My apologies, sahib. I have dialed the incorrect extension," and then snigger with delight before replacing the handset.

More practical for the busy employee than telephone *kama* is e-mail *kama.* Silent, stealthy, yet rife with seductive charm, e-mail allows the frail wallflower to blossom into a saucy charmer, sending sweet missives to dance before the eyes of the beloved. Soon the chiming of the e-mail announcement brings a rosy glow of anticipation to the recipient's cheeks. She rolls her mouse coyly toward the icon, one hand poised atop the alt and tab keys, ready to toggle to another screen in case an unwanted visitor should approach. One click and the words appear, silent music to her ears like a serenade whispered into the night. Yes, there is an attachment.

In the privacy of one's own home, e-mail love may be overtly amorous or, as is well documented,

crude and even pornographic. At the office, however, the e-mail arts (*kalā*) are far more subtle, a game to be played only by the most skillful. Courtesans spend months learning the nuances of e-mail *kama,* and it is not to be undertaken lightly. Before sending an e-mail, one must imagine not only the beloved's longing glance, but also the human-resources director's chilly stare scrutinizing each phrase for impropriety, the information-technology professional's filtering device scanning for forbidden words, and one's heartfelt correspondence being forwarded company-wide by accident or malice. As when teaching parrots and mynah birds to talk, and for many of the same reasons, in no case should *rod, pudenda, jugs,* or other such explicit terms be used in e-mail, lest recipients of tender constitution become intimidated and rendered unapproachable. Consider such alternatives as, "Your fiery sword calms the incessant tickle in my sanctuary of Eros as no other." The accomplished seducer conveys promised pleasures with nary a flicker of unseemly language. Those who lack finesse write, "I have the Johnson report ready to go. It's huge. Come by and I'll give it to you," while those whose methods are refined type, "That which you desire most is here, ample and awaiting your attention."

Once a successful liaison has been established, e-mail offers boundless opportunities for scintillation. Teasing, taunting, one drives desire to a maniacal extreme during the course of the day. As in the act itself, the best approach is varied in tempo. First, one replies immediately, words charged with zeal. Next, one waits an agonizing hour or more to respond, as if occupied with a pressing task or important conference call. Next, one sharpens the sword of wit, lacing each sentence with crafty double entendres and daring the recipient to ponder its true meaning. When e-mailing a group about a business matter, the daring may insert an inside joke only the intended will understand.

Most difficult of all is the progress-oriented response to a message that may or may not be an invitation to saunter among the fragrant weeds beyond the village. The following anecdote is instructive. A nobleman received an e-mail from a beautiful courtesan down the hall, which read only "69 is fine." Surely her intentions were salacious, but the nobleman dared not overstep the bounds of courtesy. Weighing his words as though they were so much gold, he composed the following reply after much deliberation: "Also fine with me." Predictably, nothing ever came of it, though he realized later that she was referring to his suggestion that she reduce her budget of 76 rupees by 10 percent, making it roughly 69. The point is, had he not been incapacitated by nerves, he might have used her missive—which, though legitimate enough, plainly smacked of flirtation—to embark on a few saucy rounds of back and forth, perhaps culminating in a rendezvous. Still, considering his awkwardness in the medium, his judicious restraint may have been prudent.

E-mail can also be used to identify prospective lovers. Like the distribution of snacks and supplies in one's office, forwarding the occasional pleasantry to a roster of acquaintances provides an opportunity for potential lovers to respond with flirtatious banter, betraying their hidden aspirations. Though the powers of e-mail are great, one must never attempt to compel affection through magical e-mail practices described in occult texts, as this will undermine trust and make harmonious relations impossible in the long term.

In the Event of Rejection

Due to the delicate nature of union, especially while at the office, rejection may occur even if one is handsome, intelligent, successful, well groomed, diligent, and skillful in the 40 Ways. This may take place if the beloved is in a state of denial due to an ethical obligation to remain faithful to his or her current lover, husband, or courtesan. The other times it occurs include when the beloved has been inappropriately flirtatious without serious intentions, or when the lover has developed an irrational

Clearly the Crush is Unwelcome

attachment without just provocation. It may also occur due to an oversight in judgment brought about by fatigue or imbibing fermented beverages. Thus it is said that drinking fermented liquors with coworkers while smitten is like walking barefoot through a junk heap of broken pottery. A loose tongue and lewd eye often lead to disaster.

If the suitor betrays his or her interest in copulation and the desired party is visibly repulsed, clearly the crush is unwelcome. Repulsion can be recognized by the display of a grotesque expression, the upper lip snarled in disgust, the body leaning as far away from the suitor as possible, or the breath hissing from the nostrils like steam. In such cases, the suitor must immediately retreat, coughing uncontrollably and feigning illness such as dizziness, headache, weak stomach, or gout. Later, out of sympathy, the love object may take pity and say nothing of the incident, pretending it never happened. If asked, the suitor should deny having shown any romantic interest in the offended party, stating total ignorance of any such event, and should observe the 90 Days, having as little contact with the formerly beloved as possible. He or she should refrain from phoning, sending e-mail, composing poetry on palm leaves, or sending endearing statuary of geese and goats. The suitor must go so far as to purport total disinterest, even convincing one's own self that the gesture was never made, but was in fact an innocent remark misinterpreted as an invitation to copulate.

Should rumors of humiliation linger, the suitor must parade evidence of a preexisting fully committed relationship each Monday morning. He or she must seize opportunities to share stories of happy weekend outings, evenings at the theater, and tender exchanges with the imaginary lover. If flowers and telegrams can be sent convincingly, this should be arranged.

Using Go-Betweens and Messengers

An excellent means of avoiding failure as described above is to employ the services of a go-between, which may be a mutual acquaintance, assistant, courtesan, or servant, but not one's mother or aunt. The go-between must befriend the beloved, gaining his or her trust and singing the praises of the lover.

In this way, the go-between learns the mood of the beloved, and whether or not the love light shines favorably on the suitor. The go-between should be selected carefully, bearing in mind that betrayal is not out of the question. If one's lover is tender like a doe, with skin like velvet and lips like the flesh of ripe cherries, and the go-between is a womanizing brute reputed to lay his lips on the palm of every doe he meets, or if he is unsurpassed in beauty and skilled in the 40 Ways, and in addition is well spoken and admired by all, not to mention a practiced

The Go-Between

lutenist with a voice like melted honey, then he may steal the beloved for his own pleasure, whether by intention or accident. Conversely, if there is a youthful manager with slender legs, a scent like blooming jasmine, and eyes as black as Shiva's chest hair, she should not be sent to the beloved bearing erotic tidings. If no suitable go-between is available and access to the beloved is tricky, the hero or heroine should seek out the occupant of a cubicle adjacent to the lover's and become fast friends. Visiting the neighbor frequently and often speaking of one's stoic loneliness and selfless goodwill to others within hearing of the beloved, one may be gradually accepted into his or her tender consideration.

Making the Acquaintance of a Potential Lover

Employees should accept all invitations to lunch in small, festive groups, though not with the same group more than once a week, and should cultivate the habit of casually inviting others to join the group, so as to eventually invite the object of affection without nervousness or deliberation. After

Lunching on a Grassy Hillock

lunching in a group including the precious boy or girl on numerous occasions, familiarity is firmly established and it is acceptable to suggest lunch together, without specifying that solitude is the aim, even if it is so. The couple should lunch on a grassy hillock under a shade tree, telling amusing personal stories to each other while they nibble their repast. If all is well and the unsuspecting boy or girl is relaxed, inclined on the grass with a smiling face and the shoes removed, the lover should hum a whimsical tune and touch the girl's or boy's fingertips as though in friendship. If all continues well, the lover must scratch the big toe of the apparently willing boy or girl, as though by accident, with his or her own toe, and gaze with obvious intent into the beloved's eyes. If all is still well, the lovers will embrace, sigh, scratch and bite each other's ears and necks, and pinch the flesh of their forearms until they are covered in goosebumps. Then they should return quickly to the office, parting swiftly and speaking as little as possible.

Soon the lovers, having made dinner plans, may wish to leave the office together. To escape watchful eyes, they must choose a spot near the office but not on the paths habitually tread by coworkers. It should be a place where one might linger normally, such as a bus stop, rose garden, bookstore, or falafel cart. Having arranged a meeting time by e-mail or phone, one worker loudly proclaims his or her intention to go home, bidding farewell to all. The other should remain behind, making him- or herself conspicuous by yawning rudely or making photocopies. After ten to fifteen minutes, he or she may depart respectably for the rendezvous. Should one or more coworkers attach themselves to the departing lover, saying "We'll walk out with you," great care must be taken to shake the hangers-on before reaching the rendezvous point. If they prove unreasonable, the lover should pretend to have forgotten something back at the office, ideally an electronic file for which one must reboot or a poultice which must be pounded out slowly from stiff cane.

More arduous is a tandem departure from a work-related function or party. Such departures are known to inspire lasting gossip and must be arranged artfully. If one of the lovers possesses a carriage, ricksha, litter, or van, then he or she must seize control of the situation. Rising to leave, the driver should offer to take home any who require a lift, addressing this option in particular to a friend, an acquaintance, and a total stranger, in that order. Only then should the driver extend the offer to the beloved, who must accept. Contriving various persuasive arguments, the driver must be certain that the beloved is the last to be deposited at home. In acute circumstances, as when one overly polite rider insists on being dropped last, the driver must suggest an activity certain to be unappealing to the rider, for which the beloved will express mock enthusiasm. Examples include delousing pets or livestock, visiting a local plumbing supply store, driving a great distance to an uninteresting place, or stopping at a vegan living-foods restaurant for a late meal. Whatever the ruse, it should be contrived to arouse certain displeasure in the rider.

Holiday parties are perhaps the best, and riskiest, venue for seduction offered by corporate institutions. Spirits are high, fermented beverages abound, and employees adorn themselves in their most elegant clothing and jewelry. The codes of behavior unravel as the night progresses, until formerly reserved sales managers and Web site technicians hit the dance floor like a cartload of grapes jiggling down a bumpy road. At such events, timing

Sharing a Taxi Home from the Holiday Party

is everything. One must sniff out the precise moment, just before the party crests the summit of amusement, to convince the beloved to leave the party and share a taxi home. It does not matter if others come along, so long as they are the first to be dropped off. If they attempt to remain in the cab, one should proceed to dampen the jovial atmosphere by discussing work, resorting even to annual goals, sales targets, legal concerns, and other stressful topics until the unwanted riders flee. Once alone, the lover embraces the beloved passionately. He or she nibbles the ears, kisses the nose or chin, and grazes the other's cheeks with his or her own eyelashes. If a ride of more than ten blocks remains, further embraces such as rifling the breasts and snogging like badgers in a den are expected.

The Walk of Shame

Assuming all goes according to the heart's aspirations at a swifter pace than anticipated, the warming rays of dawn will shine upon two lovers' limbs entwined in a peaceful embrace. Surely they have slept late, intoxicated by the nectar of intimacy. Jolting upright, they stare at the clock. Eight-fifty, and they must be at work within the hour. Panic seizes them. The heroine gathers her sari and sandals, rushing through her morning toilette, cringing at the prospect of the walk of shame. Surely everyone will remember she wore this sari yesterday. Surely they will put two and two together. The boy tries to help, pointlessly offering her his collection of tunics and Oxford shirts, loafers and khakis.

Realistically, the girl has three options. She can send a message to work saying she is ill and bedridden, and in doing so sully herself with the soil of dishonesty. She can bribe or seduce a local dry cleaner, persuading the proprietor to lend her a sari left for cleaning and pressing. Or she can snatch one of her lover's shirts, step into it, and tie the sleeves around her waist in the Japanese obi-belt fashion to make an impromptu skirt. If none of these options appeals, she must arrive at work in the previous day's costume, suffering the sidelong glances and whispers of girlfriends and bosses. Lovers are wise to travel prepared for such emergencies, packing tooth powder and hair oil in their briefcase and dressing in layers, which can be rearranged to simulate a change of ensemble. Another useful strategy is to do as northerners do, and occasionally wear the same clothes twice or even three times each week, declaring loudly the economy and smart thinking of such a practice. Thus, when in need, a favorable precedent will have been set.

The Walk of Shame

If they are to keep their romance a secret, the lovers must be vigilant, always separating after leaving the house or apartment in order to stagger their arrival at the office, and even taking separate buses or trains if necessary. They must prepare for inquiries should they be spotted on incongruous modes of transport. Imagine rubbing elbows with a coworker on the morning commute. The glance travels from hero to heroine, the mind works. "Does he not live in New Jersey? Why, then, is he riding in from Brooklyn with Henderson? Wait a second, Henderson just got that new place in Williamsburg." And soon the lovers are found out. The smallest detail—a telltale coffee cup from the wrong neighborhood—can give their secret away.

Holidays and anniversaries pose further challenges. As tradition dictates, one must honor the beloved with gifts and pleasant sayings on the day of Saint Valentine, the day of birth, the spring and autumnal equinoxes, and other such occasions; however, any special attention will make evident the unique bond the couple shares. Yet if one does not send flowers or offer candies and dazzling trinkets, the beloved may feel neglected and turn a chilly flank in the sack. The solution is as clear as dew on a white rose: One must send gifts under an assumed name. The name itself may be crafted in such a way as to betray the true bearer only to the beloved. If the beauty enjoys the exercises described in the sage Dattaka's famed erotic manifesto, then the name her admirer adopts for sending such gifts as licorice, pomegranates, and jars of preserved lemon rind should be Akattad. Or if a girl rides a horse across the desert at night to meet her chosen one, then, when sending flowers or candy at the office, she may sign her name The Stallion Who Rides in Darkness. Such is the manner of conduct appropriate to two persons engaged in an illicit affair at the office.

PART FOUR

The 40 Ways

For millennia, scholars have referred to the 40 Ways, which number more than 40 but are practiced during the 40-hour work week and so are termed the 40 Ways. This text addresses the most accepted and accessible, leaving to other volumes the bizarre practices of deviants and foreigners.

The pineapple is renowned for its golden fruit and sweet nectar, yet if a greedy diner recklessly bites into its prickly skin before it has been properly sliced, the experience is far from gourmet. Similarly, the yoni or lingam yields up its famous pleasures only to the patient student of the 40 Ways. One must not assault the yoni or lingam without preliminary love play. And though there are many fashions of making love, the masters agree: when it comes to the subject of caresses, nibbles, and amorous games, more is better. Happily, many common office supplies can be employed to stimulate interest.

Dance of a Thousand Sticky Notes

A favorite early love game of office workers is the Dance of a Thousand Sticky Notes. Like the Dance of the Seven Veils, the body is hidden behind many colorful layers. With swaying arms and hips that shimmy, slowly the dancer removes the sticky notes, one by one, first uncovering a seductive shoulder, next revealing the tender cavern of the navel, and so on faster and faster until the lust for direct contact of flesh upon flesh can no longer be resisted.

Titillating Uses of Handy Supplies and Hardware

Traditionally, prior to coition, kneading and suckling the breasts and thighs is practiced. If a lover uses the rolling ball of the mouse to massage in a circular motion, it is called "kneading dough with a rodent." If the 20 erotic pressure points located at the temples, wrists, ankles, elbows, knees, thighs, haunches, armpits, collarbone, and earlobes are stimulated using the eraser of a pencil, it is called "the happy tramp of the wayward beetle." An ardent lover may also draw a cable, whether USB or standard, over the length of the body in a titillating manner as though it were an ostrich feather, raising gooseflesh and stimulating the centers of pleasure.

Kneading Dough with a Rodent

The Scotsman's Rite

When the lover's cheeks are aflame and the lips yearn for kisses, still it is not time to consummate desire. Far from it. The sensations which lie ahead may include such games as the Scotsman's Rite. Unfurling a length of tape, the lover presses his (or her) thighs against the beloved and applies a transparent adhesive strip along the forearm in one sensuous stroke. Taunting, writhing, with copious sniggering and gestures of cruel warning, the lover builds anticipation to a feverish pitch before deftly ripping away the tape with an unbridled yank. Titillated, mildly injured in a pleasurable fashion, the beloved sets her (or his) mind on amorous retaliation. The same can be practiced using bandages or medical tape from the first-aid box. Advanced practitioners with an appetite for the extreme where pain and pleasure mingle should use packing tape.

Stamping and drawing, like judicious biting and scratching, are as essential to office *kama* as pinches, tweaks, slaps, and accompanying sighs. One must not fail to take up a favorite pen and gingerly trace a landscape of idyllic beauty or transcribe an appropriate passage from an epic poem on the backside of the beloved. Even the numbers from a year-end sales report, if artfully rendered, will quicken the pulse. A winning technique begins with an ordinary paper clip, unfolded to make an ideal scratching tool called "the lion's claw." Seated in a comfortable chair not more than 48 inches from the computer monitor, the lover flings the beloved over his or her lap and commences to lightly drag the lion's claw over the golden expanse of flesh, tracing spirals, fruits, and long tendrils of jasmine up and down the body; marking a place for a kiss or pinch; and finally pausing to etch a commemorative half-moon into the shoulder blade with the thumbnail. Thus are the carnal practices of barbarians and wild beasts put to good use.

In regard to stamping, the lover should not refrain if the moment and setting recommend it. In some regions, stamping is considered stimulating, while in others it is offensive. The lover should conform to his or her companion's preference. Today's Date, Paid, Received, and Confidential are all acceptable and serve as souvenirs of the encounter for several days afterward. One must begin at the toes and work upward, stamping, biting, and licking like an obsessed bureaucrat.

Sensuous Rain of Packing Popcorn

Some otherwise commendable techniques, such as shampooing the toes, calves, and thighs with fragrant bubbly soaps, are impractical at the office and should be avoided. An acceptable substitute is "the sensuous rain of packing popcorn." One lover seats the other in a comfortable chair and binds his or her hands behind the back of the chair. The lover still at liberty then fashions a blindfold from two floppy disks and adhesive tape, secures it in place, and jogs down to the mail room in search of packing materials. Upon his or her return, the tender blossom, bound and blindfolded, trembles with anticipation. Standing above, the lover charged momentarily with the leadership role sprinkles packing popcorns over the innocent darling's quivering body, allowing the tiny bits of clingy puffed organic matter or polystyrene to cascade and tumble over the naked flesh. When the box is empty, the lover winds a sheaf of bubble wrap around the beloved's chest and hips and leaps astride. Together they thrill to a cacophony of explosive pops.

A Cacophony of Explosive Pops

Desktop Commerce

The desktop environment, though hardly a cushioned dais strewn with pillows and silken draperies, is entirely suited to congress as long as both lovers are in the grip of a feverish passion and are sufficiently limber. The computer monitor is good for anchoring firmly between the legs when bending backward or forward; like a sturdy scanner tray, the keyboard tray offers an impromptu massage to the recumbent partner; and a closed laptop or dictionary makes a trusty support for raising the hips.

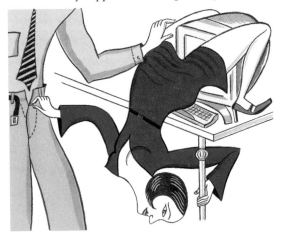

Advanced Prowess

The Spin and Other Seated Positions

Any ordinary chair will serve a lover well, especially if he or she masters the inverted positions, with legs flung over the back support. Once this is accomplished, the lucky duo can proceed to more advanced maneuvers. With the two lovers fitted together like yin and yang, yin reclines while yang pushes off the floor to keep the couple twirling round and round in an arabesque of amour to make "two love-struck scarabs on a spinning leaf."

Far simpler for novices or those prone to motion sickness is "congress between two diplomats," in which the lingam wielder sits in the chair with both feet flat on the floor and the yoni bearer is astraddle, legs resting comfortably on the armrests. Manipulating the lever under the seat, the lingam wielder deftly raises and lowers the chair in timed unison with the undulation of the flesh. Up, down. Up, down. Those with truly advanced prowess may choose to spin and recline simultaneously as well.

Ergonomically Correct Congress

Depending on how often the workers dwell in the temple of love, and how long they stay each time, they may need to practice ergonomically correct congress in order to avoid injury. The lovers should take accurate measurements in order to determine the best possible positioning of yoni and lingam. First, they should measure the distance from the bottom of the scrotum to the top of the head, and from the entrance to Shiva's cave to the tip of the chin. Taking the difference between the two distances and multiplying by pi, they arrive at the appropriate angle for penetration, in radians. It is extremely important that this angle be maintained at all times, even if severe discomfort results. (Note that in the case of lingam-free love, no measurements are necessary, but the lovers' limbs, heads, and torsos should always be held at perfect 45- or 90-degree angles to each other.) The chair may be tilted, raised, or lowered to accommodate the angle while seated, and an ergonomically enhanced keyboard may be necessary.

Positions Typically Favored by the General Populace

Of standard positions, several are preferred, including "lentils and rice," when the two lovers rub together and twine limbs until they are as deeply intermingled as a mélange of grains and legumes. If a lingam wielder sits atop a two-drawer filing cabinet and a yoni bearer mounts him nose to nose and casts her legs over his shoulders, they are "two monkeys climbing a gum tree." If one of the lovers grips the computer monitor between silken thighs and reclines backward over the keyboard, and the other leans forward as though to touch his or her forehead to the desktop and stays there some time, it is called "tempting the gods of occupational safety." When one lover types a memo while the other performs unmentionable tasks in order to distract him or her, it is called "the determined mollusk pestered by a jellyfish with plenty of tentacles." Another popular practice, "polishing the mahogany," refers to congress while one party is seated on the conference room table.

More Titillating Uses of Handy Supplies

In practicing office *kama,* lovers should strive to be resourceful, utilizing all that is available to them. Shredded paper, for example, makes an effective and punishing cat-o'-nine-tails. In the absence of henna, permanent markers can be used to decorate the lover's hands and feet, or to leave sentimental tattoos or shameful suggestions penned in secret places. Mail-room personnel often complain that their gummy finger-cots don't last more than a week before vanishing. Has no office manager or mail clerk discovered their secondary use? While it is true that they facilitate the handling of paper products, in amorous play they are used to increase friction when noodling the stone at the entrance to Cupid's grotto (*bhāgānhkura*). Earplugs heighten the sensation of touch as much as a blindfold does, and rubber bands can be used for a variety of erotic purposes, including ritualistic snapping and buttressing the lingam and cullions together at the base. Paper clips on the earlobes, pinkie fingers, and other sensitive areas drive the chaste into a frenzy.

Before or after hours of rambunctious love-making, one may wish to pamper the lover with a massage and pedicure. In such instances, all-purpose correction fluid serves well as nail polish, and can also be used to make fetching *bindi* dots.

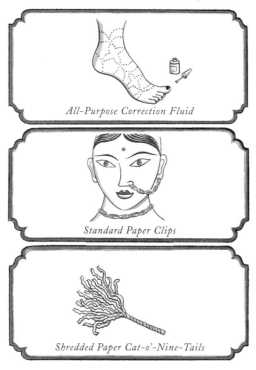

All-Purpose Correction Fluid

Standard Paper Clips

Shredded Paper Cat-o'-Nine-Tails

The Quickie

Lovers who wish for more privacy should arrange to meet in a supply or server room, stairwell, elevator, bathroom, or other secluded retreat. Such breathless encounters require skill and planning, as opportunity must be swiftly seized, and often while standing. There may only be time for a few caresses to set the mood, an embrace or two, and, at best, one or two dozen expedient thrusts, so the lovers must be ready. Such well-known positions as "the camel and jockey," "the wild boar couple who care nothing for appearances," and "two colorful kites meeting in the air" are all good for speedy congress in tight quarters.

Solo Congress

Despite planning, there are certain to be periods of abstinence for even the most dedicated student of the 40 Ways. Perhaps the office has experienced too little turnover and all appropriate matches have been exhausted. Or, one may be refraining from relations for spiritual reasons. At other times, due to the heartless whimsy of the gods or a defective mojo, one is alone, filled with useless desire and feeling repugnant, like a baboon. Or else one has a lover, but is separated from him or her. In other cases, lust runs too forcefully in the blood and the paltry hours between morning congress and congress before sleeping are too long to endure. In all such circumstances, solo congress is the answer.

Solo congress (*simhākrānta,* or "seizing the lion") can be practiced at the office in a multitude of ways, with or without clothing, in front of others or privately, even—for those with advanced skills— during meetings. Naturally, it is important to be discreet. Most companies have done away with the masturbatoriums of old, and today employees must make do with whatever impromptu arrangements they can manage on their own. Still, moaning, twitching convulsively, and crying out, no matter how tempting and seemingly harmless, are almost always inappropriate. Writhing under one's desk and rubbing against invitingly soft cubicle walls are equally ill-considered and should not be practiced except at times of extreme vexation, and then only when one is certain all other employees and janitorial services personnel have departed for the day.

Barring those that cause a stir among coworkers, any technique that drives the proverbial herd of llamas over the ridge is to be deemed successful, even if it is unconventional, and should be added to one's personal repertoire. Those who are inexperienced or excessively shy or morose in temperament, and have thus failed to develop an adequate repertoire of solo congress options, should select one of the following techniques to achieve their goal. When a female worker stands beside a desk chair with one leg cast over the armrest, which has been raised as high as possible, and pretends to be listening to her coworker while mindlessly rocking back and forth, solo congress is in progress. When a female worker stands at the electric pencil sharpener, leaning into it with the hips, and sharpens for an unreasonably long time, or else sharpens an unnecessary plethora of pencils, all the while stroking and rubbing the sharpener as it hums and grinds away, it is called "the dream of the quivering wooden shaft." When a male worker carries a stress-relieving toy in his pocket for several hours, squeezing it constantly and muttering softly to himself, he is surely practicing solo congress. When a worker lingers in a bathroom stall long after expelling evil matter, it is solo congress. Further, when a worker politely sets his or her mobile phone to vibrate instead of ring during a meeting, and yet does not answer the phone despite many calls, he or she is "scaling the glistening slopes of Nanda Devi without a guide."

Solo Congress

Role Play

For neophytes, sneaking kisses in the hallway, touching fingertips or toes under the conference room table, and sharing nan at lunchtime are enough to keep the heart prancing like a dik-dik. The veteran, however, will require more for satisfaction. Role-playing will take travelers far down the golden road to nirvana, even if their union is insipid, like poorly seasoned masala. Some lovers may feel a secret desire to dominate their partners, saying, "Can I see you in my office?" and later, "Close the door, please." They may demand to be called Mr. President, Madam Prime Minister, Chancellor, Viscount, Her Majesty, or Governor. Others long to return to the submissive state of childhood, saying, "What can I do? My computer has crashed without explanation and I am in need of assistance." If a corner office is vacant, lovers can take turns playing CEO and his or her devoted underling. It will be seen that some CEOs are gentle but firm; others are vile brutes. A lover who relieves the supply cabinet of the first-aid kit has set the stage for a doctor's visit to his or her favorite patient.

Remote Congress

If the organization has offices in several regions and the lovers are occasionally separated, there may be the opportunity for video conference congress. If this is not feasible, a trusted messenger or courtesan may be used to ferry erotic poetry back and forth between the separated lovers. If one of the lovers has a pager or other PDA, suggestive text should be sent, timed to arrive during interminable presentations and board meetings, when the mind is inclined to wander. At other times of separation, the office photocopier, scanner, and fax machine are like so much clay in a master sculptor's hands, with endless possibilities.

Advanced Techniques

With years of practice, lovers may attain a level of proficiency which enables them to attempt more advanced positions and techniques, such as the "rolling hand-truck embrace" and the "magic carpet ride" (this usually requires the assistance of at least two strong eunuchs). A favorite among senior officials from Jaipur to Sri Lanka is the "rabbit and the ass" (congress while one party discusses important business matters on phone). Another is the "hanging fern grotto embrace" (extremely advanced), in which one party is lowered from an exposed overhead heating duct or fluorescent light fixture. Other advanced techniques involve three-way conference calling, multiple-party video conferencing, and carpool or ride-share congress.

Hanging Fern Grotto Embrace

PART FIVE

Comportment in the Face of Adversity

Professionals in all fields must maintain their dignity, and office *kama*, even when practiced artfully, can pose a challenge to anyone's composure. Engaged in the removal of shrewdly positioned sticky notes from one's partner with the teeth and lips, the startled lover looks up to discover a team of engineers come by for the weekly status update. Surely the moment is spoiled and pleasure jeopardized, but all is not lost if the lover remains calm and begins the meeting without fanfare. In many cases, the impropriety will go unnoticed and business continue as usual. Still, professionals should take precautions to avoid being interrupted while entertaining a guest. For an office, precautions may include installing a heavy bolt lock, playing loud music, drawing heavy curtains, and taping a note to

Surely the Moment is Spoiled

the outside of one's door reading, "Do not disturb. Working." If it is impractical to play music loudly enough to cover the sounds of gleeful delectation, a recording of waves crashing, flowing water, a rainstorm, aircraft engines, traffic on a multilane freeway, or other innocuous white noise should be employed.

In Case of Discord

It is important to maintain a harmonious rapport with one's lovers, lest a sassy remark muttered in anger betray all to one's colleagues, promoting undignified gossip. Telling remarks, derogatory or otherwise, should be greeted with a bemused expression and, if possible, a friendly and amusing retort. With luck, a cleansing round of chortling will follow. A more serious outburst, such as shouting, crying, or the throwing of one's files onto the floor and the subsequent kicking of them down the hallway, is more difficult to disguise. This is a good time to take a very long lunch break.

Changing Lovers within the Office

If it becomes necessary to change lovers within the office, one should avoid selecting a member of the same team or department as either oneself or the current lover, lest complications arise. Whenever possible, one should observe the 90 Days of aloofness in between lovers, fasting for the first three weeks. If it is unfeasible to observe the 90 Days, lovers should send their current romance a fresh fig leaf, or bar of chocolate, perforated with bite marks all the way around, signifying the abrupt end of a passionate affair. At the same time, they should send a beautifully wrapped, radiant white marshmallow with one pristine bite out of it to the new love, signifying the unbridled passion bursting from the depths of the soul.

Bar of Chocolate   *Fig Leaf*   *Marshmallow*

Cheap Muslin in a Sandstorm

Fig leaves (or chocolate bars, see above) can bring opportunity as well as the agony of spurned love. When an associate sends the bitten fig leaf to his or her lover, and it is obvious to all that the discarded party is torn asunder like so much cheap muslin in a sandstorm, then it may be possible to assume the former lover's role without observing the 90 Days.

In fact, the distraught creature will generally welcome the comfort and intrigue of a new liaison. This is called "lighting the lantern already filled with oil by another," or the "art of the retread."

If there are lovers who send the bitten fig leaf, so there must be recipients. Oh, unlucky victims! How their pain rends the heart like a palm uprooted by a foraging elephant's tusks! Those on the receiving end of the marred foliage will feel their eyes fill with tears like water gushing from a cistern. They may see stars, and their lips tremble with agonized disbelief. Their first impulse is to shriek and tear their hair, hurl the betrayer's gifts out the nearest window, and grind the flowers and incense so recently appreciated into the industrial carpet until nothing but a bitter smudge remains. This, however, is not the judicious path. Seizing the steadying pillar of decorum and tossing the leaf back into its manila envelope, the wiser lover, though equally spurned and heartbroken, speaks only of quarterly goals, action points, high-level concepts, and supply-chain management. The model of poise and efficiency, he or she turns to career opportunities with a renewed hunger for success. At the finish of the day, instead of imbibing

The Heroic Creature Stops at the Gym

fermented drinks and sobbing hysterically, this heroic creature stops at the gym to tone the body's muscles and release tension before heading home for a healthful meal and a good rest. The next day, noting that the bitten greenery has only improved the luster of the discarded pearl, the former romance experiences regret and curses the impulse that made him or her sink hasty molars into the symbolic plant. The spurned lover must maintain stellar comportment at all times. Eventually, an opportunity to publicly confess the former lover's most damning weakness will arise and should be quietly seized out of spite, though kindly and respectfully understated. Possible weaknesses include cruelty to one's aged parents, dislike for pets and children, stinginess, repellent hygienic practices, emotional instability, and a woefully inadequate mastery of the 40 Ways.

Resuming Neutrality

If the parting of two entwined bodies is mutually agreed upon, matters are less complex. One observes the 90 Days of discreet separation and then resumes amicable relations of friendship, taking care not to refer to the past romance in the presence of coworkers. The lovers must cultivate a positive view of the affair and their friendship, and keep all gifts and mementos they exchanged hidden in a polished sandalwood box. As a courtesy and precaution against resuming courtship involuntarily, both parties should change their hairstyles, jewelry, perfume or cologne, and the tea houses and banquet rooms they frequent. On holidays and special occasions, an affectionate gift of blended betel wrapped in a banana leaf and tied with a silk cord is appropriate.

In the Event of Unwanted Affection

Of other romantic difficulties at the office, there are many upon which the sages pontificate. Foremost of these is the unreciprocated crush. Not as painful as outward rejection, it is nevertheless agonizing for both parties and can continue for years if left unchecked. Beginning as pals, before long one traveler tumbles down the bumpy slope of love. Eventually, he or she plucks up the courage to declare unfettered devotion; the situation is serious. There is only one course, and it is not delicate. The beloved party must make him- or herself utterly abhorrent for a period of not less than 12 and not more than 16 days and nights. They must cease to bathe and coif themselves; ladies must not launder the sari; gentlemen should allow their beards and mustaches to range over the face unkempt and even curl into their ears and mouth, trapping bits of food and lint; they must expel sordid wind from all orifices with unrestrained blasts, and without apology; they should pick and scratch liberally, inspecting and then ejecting the detritus collected under the nails; they must voice asinine opinions in meetings; they must even essay to appear ungracious, like a cretin, and ride a lame camel to work. Thus the enchantment is broken without grief.

The Beloved Makes Herself Abhorrent

On Moderation and Forbidden Acts

In regard to self-control, moderation, diplomacy, and the 40 Ways, a wise businessman once said, "Man, stroke the creamy thighs of your coworker with vigilance! Be liberal and clever. Do not be coarse, or you will find yourself like the lover of Indra, wife of Gautama, whose testicles fell to the ground like two walnuts when the great sage cursed his philandering exploits."

According to the sages, there are five forbidden acts of office *kama,* two ill-advised, and one to be generally avoided. Together they constitute the eight practices unworthy of genteel lovers. The five forbidden acts are:

§ Seducing the husband or wife of a coworker at the office holiday party
§ Seducing a man or woman openly acknowledged to be involved with a widely known and respected third party
§ Seducing the love object of a close associate or friend, regardless of the status or potential of the infatuation

§ Taking multiple secret lovers simultaneously in the same office
§ Sharing unseemly and mortifyingly specific romantic details about a coworker with other coworkers

The two ill-advised acts are:
§ Firing, demoting, or otherwise using one's position to torment or damage a former lover or the former lover of an associate of whom one is fond
§ Attempting to seduce employees in a serial fashion, shamefully progressing from one desk to the next until successful

The last act to be generally avoided is:
§ Persuading a lover to assume one's most tedious responsibilities, such as data entry, budget forecasting, proofreading, millet husking, and dismissing inferior servants or managers

Certainly, restraint is necessary, especially when one can never predict where or when the fateful dart of love will find its mark. Thankfully, there are also four recommended practices said to lead to good fortune, luck, and long life. They are:

§ Falling in love with the sibling of the boss's husband or wife, or the sibling of an important vendor

§ Falling in love with one recently heartbroken by another

§ Speaking well of former lovers and finding them jobs in other offices

§ Engaging in group sex or amorous games (*abhimāni*) with members of a team or work group, in order to improve communication and understanding of interdependencies

Rekindling a Cooling Fire

Seldom are magical practices advised by the prudent, but in the event of flagging devotion to the erotic arts at work, certain aphrodisiacal practices and potions serve to invigorate the senses without risk of harm. First and foremost, the afflicted must surround themselves with images and iconography of virile beasts, such as tigers, bull elephants, wild stallions, investment bankers, venture capitalists, stuntpersons, welders, and heavy equipment operators. It may be necessary and advisable to carry a drawing of a white stallion with a formidable erection or a politician giving the "thumbs up" in one's pocket at all times. Ladies should carry a lump of moist clay to work with the fingers, and should sip fermented toddy-palm juice after hours. A key chain with a small monkey figurine will help stimulate interest for both sexes, as will visits to the park to watch dogs fornicate freely. Ginger tea and wild figs must be consumed to excess by both men and women. If none of these remedies helps a man, he must collect the sweat from a ram's testicles and rub it vigorously onto his member every night for one week. Likewise, a woman in need must gather crustaceans and other sea fruits by moonlight, brew a strong broth from their meats and juices, and massage this mixture into the yoni nightly for one week. Soon the gates of rapture will open, and ecstasy will polish the mind like vinegar shines a mirror.

Invigorating the Senses

Office Kama Sutra has presented many practices for men and women to consider. The wise will choose among them only after weighing the values of chastity, advancement, and virtue against those of passion and wanton lust. As noted in the ancient treatise of the *Kama Sutra*, "One must not go too far in the direction of the weft or woof. Success with girls is obtained by moderation." And why not with boys as well? Through virtue, moderation, and goodwill, the joys of office *kama* are made manifest, and peaceful contentment of mind and body sustained throughout one's career.